No Girls Allowed

Linda Lee Maifair

Illustrated by Meredith Johnson

MINNEAPOLIS

For my "Terrific Two" nephews,
Mark and Daniel

Cover design: Hedstrom Blessing

Library of Congress Cataloging-in-Publication Data

Maifair, Linda Lee.
   No girls allowed / by Linda Lee Maifair : illustrated by Meredith Johnson
      p.   cm. — (Ready, set, read! beginning readers)
   Summary: Alexander and Bartholomew don't want to let the new girl into their club, but she proves to be braver, smarter, and a better friend than they are.
   ISBN 0-8066-2688-7
   [1. Clubs—Fiction. 2. Haunted houses—Fiction. 3. Friendship—Fiction. 4. Conduct of life—Fiction.] I. Johnson, Meredith, ill. II. Title. III. Series.
   PZ7.M2776No   1993
[E]—dc20
                                         93-40083
                                              CIP
                                            AC

The paper in this publication meets the minimum requirements of American National Standard for Information Sciences—Permanence of Paper for Printed Library Materials, ANSI Z329.48-1984. ∞™

Manufactured in the U.S.A.   AF 9-2688
97   96   95   94   93   1   2   3   4   5   6   7   8   9   10

Contents

The New Kid

"Skateboard. Basketball hoop. No baby junk," I told Alexander. We were keeping an eye on the moving van next door.

"Wow! Look at *that*, Bart!" Alexander pointed at something in the back of the van. I never got to see what it was.

"One false move and you get it, spies!" said a tough-sounding voice behind us.

Alexander and I turned around. I was staring into the barrel of a gigantic water cannon.

What surprised me the most was the kid who was holding it. The new kid we'd been expecting since the SOLD sign went up on the house between Alexander's and old Mrs. Mulligan's. The one we prayed wouldn't be another teenager. It wasn't.

I looked at the camouflage shorts. The curly red hair. The Band-Aids on both knees. The dirty face. I stared at the Husky standing next to the kid. I swallowed the lump in my throat.

"One false move and you get it," the kid repeated. A grimy finger twitched on the trigger. The kid smiled.

I made the false move. "Aw," I said in disappointment, "you're just a dumb *girl*!" She almost drowned us.

Five minutes later, I stood in Alexander's mother's laundry room. In my underwear. Wiping the dripping water from my nose while my clothes bounced around in the dryer.

Alexander tossed our towels into the hamper. "That wasn't the smartest thing you've ever said, Bartholomew."

"If it hadn't been for your potato chips, she never would have found us," I told him. I fished my T-shirt out of the dryer. It was still damp. I put it on anyway.

"And if it wasn't for you, old Mrs. Mulligan wouldn't have sprayed us with her hose this morning, either. Celery sticks! Don't you ever eat anything quiet?" I pulled on my jeans. They were damp, too.

"It wasn't the celery," Alexander argued. "She's got The Power, just like they say."

"I'm not afraid of her," I said. It wasn't exactly true. We'd heard plenty of stories about Mrs. Mulligan. The teenagers told us she calls up spooks every midnight in that creepy old house of hers.

Of course, we never went anywhere near there at midnight. But we'd peeked into her cellar window when she wasn't home. And we'd looked in the kitchen window when she was busy in the front yard. The cellar looked like a dungeon. And there was a big black pot of *something* bubbling on the kitchen stove.

Once the teenagers dared us to climb

the ladder she'd been using to clean out her gutters. They dared us to look into her attic. They said it was full of "horrible, mysterious" things.

We never got to see them. The window was painted over. Somebody took the ladder away before we could climb back down again. We were stuck on the roof for two hours. Alexander's dad finally rescued us.

The older guys told us Mrs. Mulligan makes poison preserves. They said she uses the things she collects from the pond at the edge of our development. "*Living things*," they said. It made my skin crawl.

We never followed her to the pond. But we did see her go by with a net, lots of times. She'd come back with a bulging canvas bag slung over her shoulder. Sometimes the bag *wiggled*!

They said she had The Power. Not that I believed it. But I did kind of wonder. How did she know we were hiding in her bushes that morning? How did she always know when we were spying on her?

"Stay away from her if you know what's good for you!" the teenagers warned us. Our parents told us the same thing. They didn't mean it quite the same way.

"I told Millie Mulligan I wouldn't blame her a bit if she called the police the next time you boys bother her," my father said. "The Bible says to *love* your neighbor, not *spy* on her."

Alexander stuck his hand into the pocket of his shorts and pulled out a mangled plastic sandwich bag. Inside were the remains of a peanut butter, jelly, and banana sandwich. The dryer hadn't done it much good. The insides of the sandwich oozed out the corners of the bag.

"Well, one thing's for sure," I told him. "We can't have *her* in our club. The new kid. Right after dinner, I'll add NO GIRLS to the NO TEENAGERS sign on our clubhouse door. Agreed?"

Alexander stopped eating. "Aw, Bart, I don't know. I thought we voted to expand. More members, more dues, remember?"

I knew he was really thinking about the dog. Alexander loves dogs. He isn't allowed to have one because his little sister's allergic. That's why he's always catching some weird pet. He hides it till his parents find out and make him get rid of it.

The last one was a baby skunk he found in the woods. He hid it in the garage behind his stepfather's workbench. It might have been okay if his dad hadn't turned on the power saw.

I wrinkled up my nose, remembering. "We can't let some girl come between us. After all, who helped you clean the garage? Who kept your snapping turtle in a pan under his bed for a whole month after your dad found him in the bathtub?"

"The turtle died," Alexander said.

I made a face at him. "So? I bet *she* wouldn't have kept it for you. We don't need her. Or her dues. Or her dumb dog either. We can stay the Gruesome Twosome. Just you and me, right?"

"Well. . . ."

I didn't give him time to think it over. "Good!" I said. "We'll change the sign after dinner. You bring the paint. And, you gotta promise you won't let her wheedle her way in. Dog or no dog," I said.

"I promise," he said, though he sounded really disappointed.

We shook on it. Then we went to the kitchen to try the new specialty "Chef Alexandre" had made that morning. Chocolate chip, banana, peanut butter, raisin cookies with caramel icing. With the help of about a gallon of milk, I finally got one down. Alexander "only" ate six.

After supper we met at the clubhouse in Alexander's backyard. It was really an old chicken coop. We'd spent the summer fixing it up.

Alex brought the paint. I added NO GIRLS in big red letters to the sign on the door. I even underlined it. Twice.

I stood back and smiled in satisfaction. That took care of that!

Being Neighborly

I knocked as lightly as I could. I shifted from one foot to the other and tried not to look weird.

It wasn't easy. I had a jug of homemade vegetable soup in one hand, a fresh apple pie in the other, a loaf of long, brown bread under each arm, and a flyer about our church's ice cream social between my teeth.

"We have to be neighborly," my mother said. Then she shoved me out the door.

Mom's on the welcoming committee at church. There's nothing wrong with that. But I wind up being her delivery boy.

If she wanted to be neighborly, why didn't she take the food over herself? What would I say to Alexander if he saw me? Knocking on the new kid's back door. *With presents?*

Tap. Tap. Tap. I smiled. Nobody home after all. I started back down the porch steps. I was moving slowly, trying to juggle the soup and the pie and the bread. A thumping, scratchy sound got my attention. I turned around.

Two big eyes, a wet black nose, and a mouth full of sharp, shiny teeth stared at me out the kitchen door window. I could hear the dog mumbling at me, right through the door. It did not sound neighborly.

This time the soup didn't slow me down. I was down the walk and reaching for the gate with my elbow when I heard the laughing.

"Natasha won't hurt you," the new kid called after me. "Can't be much of a spy if you're afraid of a little dog." She opened the door a crack.

The dog stuck its nose out as far as it would go. It sort of licked its lips. If that was a "little" dog, I hated to think what a big one looked like.

"I'm not . . . not afraid. Love dogs," I said. The soggy flyer dropped out of my mouth. "I just thought nobody was home, that's all."

"There's just me and Natasha here now. Mom's at her office in the city. The housekeeper went to the grocery store. I can't let anybody in," the kid said.

"I don't want to come in," I told her. I tried to keep an eye on what I could see of the dog. "Just bringing this stuff for my mother. To welcome you to the neighborhood and invite you to church. You don't want the food, I'll take it home and eat it myself."

The door opened a little wider. I was relieved to see that the kid had a hold of the dog's collar. I hoped she was strong.

"I guess you could bring it in," the kid said. She opened the door all the way. The dog tugged at the collar.

"Uh, you hold the dog, okay? Wouldn't want it to eat . . . uh, the pie or anything," I said. I forced myself to walk back up on the porch. I edged by the dog's nose as I squeezed through the door. I decided to leave the food and get out of there. I didn't want to have anything to do with the kid or her dog.

It was the book that did me in. The book on the kitchen table where I put the pie, and the soup, and the brown bread. *Barnaby Baines and the Case of the Greedy Ghost*. One of my all-time favorites.

"*You* like Barnaby Baines?" I asked the new kid.

She nodded. "I've got all sixteen books in the series." She pointed to the book. "That's my favorite."

"Mine, too," I admitted. "I've read them all except *The Case of the Hideous Horseman*. The library never has that one when I try to get it."

"That's a good one," she said. "You'd like it. You want a piece of your mother's pie? My mother never bakes anything. She hates to cook. She won't let Mrs. Fernandez make anything good either. Says sugar makes me overactive."

I looked at the pie and sighed. My mother makes a great apple pie. "Well, maybe I could stay long enough for a small slice. To be neighborly," I said.

The girl smiled. She took two plates out of the cupboard. She plopped down on one of the kitchen stools and waved me toward the other one. Then she hacked two big hunks out of the pie and slid one onto each plate.

She picked up her piece of pie and took a big bite. The juice dribbled down through her fingers. "Good," she said, wiping at her chin with the back of her hand. "Real good."

I sat down beside her.

"What's your name?" she asked between bites.

I told her.

"You can call me Lizzie," she said, hacking out more pie.

Before I knew what I was doing, I'd helped her to finish off half the pie. She laughed at all my best dumb jokes. And we talked about every case Barnaby Baines ever solved. I even told her that I wanted to be a famous mystery writer someday. I didn't even panic much when Natasha sat up beside me and begged for the crust of my pie. I gave it to her.

"Why'd you go and shoot me with that water gun?" I asked Lizzie.

"Why'd you go and call me a dumb girl?" she wanted to know.

I apologized. So did she.

"Want to come over after supper and watch a couple of mystery stories on the VCR?" she offered. "We'll make popcorn."

I thought of Alexander. "Well. . . ."

"One's a Barnaby Baines mystery. *The Case of the Dangerous Double.*"

I groaned. Another favorite! I decided it couldn't do any harm. Alexander didn't like Barnaby Baines all that much anyway.

"Uh, sure," I said. "If my folks say it's okay." I gingerly patted Natasha on the head before I left. The copy of *The Case of the Hideous Horseman* Lizzie had loaned me was tucked under my arm.

I looked both ways to be sure no one was watching. Then I got out of there as fast as I could.

The Double-Cross

I took the long way home. I didn't want to go past Alexander's or Mrs. Mulligan's. I spent the rest of the afternoon sitting on our front porch, reading Barnaby Baines. For some reason, I couldn't concentrate very well.

Alexander came by just before dinner. "Where you been?" he asked. "I looked for you a couple of hours ago."

"Uh . . . I had to do an errand for Mom. I've been right here, reading all afternoon."

He made a face. Reading wasn't something Alexander would do on his own. Especially during summer vacation.

"Look!" He held up a huge jar. Something moved inside. "Frogs!"

Three sorry looking frogs peered out at me. "Hilda. Matilda. And Clyde," Alexander said proudly.

"How do you know?" I said. "Which is which, I mean. They all look the same to me. Green and slimy."

I looked down at the dark pants he was wearing. "What's that all over you?" I asked. "Looks like dog hair."

Alexander hesitated. "It is dog hair. I sort of ran into a dog over at the pond. By accident." He held up the jar. "Neat frogs, huh?"

I wouldn't let him change the subject. "Any dog I know?" I asked.

He looked at Hilda, Matilda, and Clyde instead of at me. "Well, now that you mention it, it was Lizzie's dog. You know, the new girl. Her name's really Elizabeth, but she likes to be called Lizzie. And. . . ."

"Alex, you promised!" I tried to look disappointed.

"I couldn't help it. The pond belongs to everybody in the development. And there she was, betting she could catch more frogs than I could. Did you know that dog can sit up, and roll over, and fetch, and. . . ." He grinned at me a little sheepishly.

"How many frogs did she catch?" I asked.

He bent over and swiped at the dog hairs that clung to his pants. "Only fourteen," he whispered into his knee.

"Fourteen!" I laughed. "And you got three? Guess you showed *her*," I said.

"You know what she's going to do with them?" he asked me. "She says she's going to put them in the washing machine. As a surprise for the housekeeper. She wants her to quit."

I remembered Mrs. Fernandez. She had come home from the store and yelled at us in two languages. I smiled. Then I cleared my throat.

Alexander and I stared at each other for a couple of seconds. Luckily, my mother called me in to dinner. Even though we were having liver, I was happy to hear her. "I gotta go," I said.

"You going to the clubhouse after supper?" Alexander asked me. He looked almost as guilty as I felt.

"Uh, no. I gotta go somewhere. Sorry."

He looked relieved. "That's okay. I'm going out, too. See you tomorrow morning?"

"Sure," I told him. "Nice frogs."

I ran inside. I even ate all my liver without complaining, so they'd let me go over to watch Barnaby Baines with Lizzie. I saved a chocolate chip cookie from dessert as a bribe for Natasha.

"Well, isn't this nice?" Lizzie's mom said when she met me. "Only her second day here, and Elizabeth's already made some new friends. My sister told me we'd like it here."

She was scraping something black and lumpy off the bottom of a pot. "Tell your mother the vegetable soup was wonderful," she said.

"You'll have to come for dinner some evening. As soon as I find a new housekeeper. We can't seem to keep them very long."

Lizzie was even better at innocent smiles than I was. She offered me some lemonade. As she handed me the glass, the doorbell rang. She went to answer it, leaving me with her mother, the burned pot, and the lemonade.

"That must be the other young man Elizabeth's invited," Mrs. Crawford said. She wiped her hands on a towel. "I'll start the popcorn."

I was just hoping she'd be better with popcorn than she'd been with their dinner when Lizzie came back into the kitchen.

She had a platter of gooey cookies in her hands.

Mrs. Crawford looked up from her popcorn popper. "I guess you two boys already know each other," she said.

We certainly did.

The Challenge

"It's not as if I *wanted* to go there," I told Alexander.

We were cleaning out the clubhouse. We never clean the clubhouse unless we're fighting about something. Then we divide it in two and bat the dirt around with a couple of old brooms.

"My mother said I had to be neighborly." I swept a pile of dust over onto Alexander's side of the room.

"I just wanted to find out if she really put the frogs in the washer," he said. He pushed the dustpile back on my side. We were getting nowhere.

"It's not like I *like* her or anything," I explained. I leaned on the handle of my broom and stared at him.

"Of course not. Me neither." He was too short to lean on the handle of his broom. He just stared back at me.

"It's still just you and me. The Gruesome Twosome, right?" I asked him. I swept the pile of dust out the door and pulled the door shut. I propped my broom up in the corner. I'd had enough cleaning, and arguing, for about a year.

"Well. . . ."

"Well what?" I said.

"I sort of mentioned to Lizzie that maybe she and the dog could visit."

"You *didn't*!" If I'd still had the broom in my hands, I would have clobbered him with it. "The dog too!"

"Makes a better mascot than a jar of frogs," Alexander pointed out.

I looked at Hilda, Matilda, and Clyde. They looked even sorrier than before.

"A dog is better protection, too. From teenagers and other pests," Alexander argued. "You can't scare anybody off with a jar of frogs."

I had to laugh. "Guess not," I said.

Knock. Tap. Tap. Knock. Somebody was at the door. Using the "secret" code.

Lizzie came in without waiting to be invited. She had a plate of brownies in her hands. The dog was right behind her. I was glad to see the brownies. She handed me the platter.

"I thought your mother didn't bake," I said.

"She doesn't." She smiled. "My aunt made those. To celebrate me joining your club and all. She's keeping an eye on me till we find a new housekeeper. She lives right. . . ."

"You aren't *in* the club yet," I interrupted. "We gotta vote first. "You'll have to wait outside till we make up our minds."

Alexander seemed surprised. Lizzie looked as if she couldn't decide whether to cry or sock me in the nose. Natasha grumbled a little in my direction.

"It's not *my* idea," I told the dog. "It's in the bylaws. Isn't that right, Alexander?"

"What bylaws? We don't have any. . . ."

I made a face at him then turned back to Lizzie. "Uh, take the dog with you, huh? Till we vote?"

"Maybe I'd better take the brownies, too," Lizzie said. "Come, Natasha! If they don't make up their minds pretty quick, we'll just eat these ourselves."

Luckily, the dog didn't need coaxing. She beat Lizzie and the brownies to the door.

"My aunt was right," Lizzie told me. "I probably don't want to join your silly club." She stomped out the door and slammed it behind her.

"Why'd you do that?" Alexander asked me.

I didn't really know. "Listen," I said, "we promised, remember. We let her in and it'll spoil everything."

"I don't see how we can keep her out. It wouldn't be very nice—not the Christian thing to do," Alexander said.

He sounded like my dad. And he was probably right. But still. . . .

"Besides, she's kinda fun. And that dog. . . ."

"Forget the dog! Lizzie said herself she's not sure she really wants to join. Suppose we give her an excuse. Suppose we tell her there's an initiation. And suppose we make the initiation so bad she changes her mind on her own. That wouldn't be our fault, would it?"

Alexander didn't look convinced. "Well. . . ."

"Of course not!" I gave him a shove toward the door. "Tell her to come back in. We decided."

Alexander shook his head at me, but he told Lizzie to come back with her dog and her brownies.

"Congratulations!" I told her. "If you pass the initiation, you're in." I took the platter out of her hands. "We'll explain it to you, as soon as we eat."

Lizzie looked at me suspiciously. "Well, I guess it won't hurt to hear what your silly initiation is. In case I decide I want to join after all," she said.

She passed out the brownies. Two for Alexander. Two for herself. Three for Natasha. One for me. I got the feeling Lizzie was trying to tell me something.

Natasha gulped down her brownies and stood with her nose about two inches from mine. I gave her the last bite of my brownie, too.

"Nice dog," I said. I patted her once, quickly. On the top of the head well back from the mouth. "I just love dogs."

I moved to the old chair on the other side of the room and watched the others finish their brownies. I wished I had another one. Lizzie's aunt was a good cook.

"Well?" Lizzie demanded when all the crumbs were gone.

"Well what?" I said.

"What do I have to do to get into your silly club?"

"Oh, that. Uh . . . well . . . I can't tell you. Not yet, that is."

"Why not?" Alexander asked.

I made another face at him. He wasn't helping a bit.

"Because it's not midnight, Alex. You know that. We can only tell the initiation at midnight. The bylaws, you know. You *do* remember the bylaws?" I nodded my head at him, hoping he'd take the hint.

He shook his head. "Seems to be a lot in those bylaws I've forgotten."

"I'm not allowed out at midnight," Lizzie said.

I smiled. "That's why we made it midnight. To see how daring you'd be. Of course, if you're afraid to sneak out and meet us here, we'll just forget the whole thing."

"I'll be here." She tilted her head to one side and raised her eyebrows at me. "Will *you?*"

I put my arm around Alexander's shoulder. "Of course we will. You can count on the Gruesome Twosome. Right, Alexander?"

"Are you kidding? I'm not allowed. . . ."

I squeezed his shoulder and gritted my teeth into a smile. "We're not afraid of anything. We'll be here waiting for you. Isn't that *right*, Alex?"

"Uh, sure," he said. "At midnight. No problem."

Lizzie, the dog, and the empty platter went back out the door. I let go of Alexander's shoulder and let out a big sigh.

"You're not allowed out at midnight either," Alexander reminded me.

"I know."

"Your dad'll. . . ."

"I *know!*" I said. I forced another smile. "Aw, there's nothing to worry about anyway. When the time comes, she'll chicken out. We'll go home before anybody even misses us. And that will be that."

"But, what if she *does* come?" Alexander asked. "You told her you'd explain the initiation at midnight. We don't *have* an initiation."

"I'll think of something." I grinned. I already had. Something so bad nobody would try it. "She's not going to come, Alex. She's just bluffing. You know that as well as I do."

I went home to a dinner I couldn't eat, even though it was lasagna, my absolute favorite.

Lizzie was waiting for us when we got back to the clubhouse at midnight. So was the dog.

The Initiation

"Well?" Lizzie said. "You gonna tell me what the initiation is or not?"

"I'm going to show you," I said. "Come on."

Two minutes later the four of us were crouching behind the hedge that divided Lizzie's yard from Mrs. Mulligan's.

"See that house?" I asked Lizzie.

"Yeah, sure. It's. . . ."

"Weird, right? Spooky old house in the middle of a modern development like this. Makes you wonder about who lives there, doesn't it?"

"Wonder what? Maybe she just likes old houses," Lizzie said. For some reason she sounded insulted.

"What about *that*?" I pointed to an upstairs window. An eerie green glow lit up the room behind the lace curtains. "What's that light doing on at a time like this? You ever see a light like that before? Probably just the sort of thing you'd use to call up spooks."

"*Spooks*?" Lizzie said. She made it sound ridiculous. "Maybe she's just got an aquarium. You know, the kind that needs a special light."

"She's got a point, Bartholomew," Alexander whispered.

This was no time for either of them to be logical. "Remember *The Case of the Moaning Mansion*?" I asked Lizzie. "Even Barnaby Baines was afraid to go into that house! Remember what *that* house looked like?"

She cocked her head to one side and stared at old Mrs. Mulligan's house for a few seconds. "A lot like this one, I guess."

"The teenagers say Mrs. Mulligan goes down to the pond and collects *things*," Alexander said. *"Living* things."

Lizzie laughed again. *"You* were down at the pond collecting living things yesterday, Alex."

Alex? Nobody called him Alex but me.

"That's different," Alexander said. "I don't go home and make poison preserves with them."

"Poison preserves?" Lizzie made it sound even more ridiculous than spooks.

"We've seen them, Lizzie. Jars and jars of them. Down in her basement," I told her. "We've looked in through the window. Lots of times."

"No wonder she squirted you with her garden hose, Bart!" Lizzie said.

I gave Alexander a sheepish grin. Nobody calls me Bart but him. Even so, he had no reason to look so insulted. *I* wasn't the one who told Lizzie about the garden hose.

"She's got The Power. Everybody says so," I said, getting back to Mrs. Mulligan again. "She makes poison preserves and potions. And she can call up spooks. And she hates kids."

Lizzie wasn't nearly as impressed, or scared, as I thought she'd be. She thought it was very funny. "Maybe you should just leave her alone. She's probably just somebody's aunt or something." She giggled. "What's this got to do with joining your silly club anyway?"

"Well," I said, "anybody who wants to join has to be brave. Brave enough to walk right up there on Mrs. Mulligan's porch. . . ."

Alexander's mouth fell open.

". . .and knock on her door. . . ."

Alexander sort of gasped.

". . .and get inside. . . ."

Alexander looked like he was going to throw up.

I smiled. "And stay in there for fifteen minutes. No matter what!"

Alexander whistled under his breath.

"That's it?" Lizzie asked. She didn't seem worried.

"Uh, yeah. I mean nobody goes into old Mrs. Mulligan's and lives to tell about it, you know. So, if you don't want to try it, we understand."

Lizzie stood up. "No sweat," she said. "Come on."

"*Now?*" I said. "In the dark?"

"Why not? You are coming with me, aren't you?"

"*No!*" Alexander and I said at the same time.

"I mean, uh . . . of course not," I said. "You gotta do it by yourself. Otherwise it doesn't count."

"Bart," Alexander said, pointing toward Mrs. Mulligan's house. His eyes were big and round. I turned around. A light was on in Mrs. Mulligan's front room. I almost fainted when the door started to open.

"Let's get out of here!" I said.

"But what about the initiation?" Lizzie asked.

"Tomorrow," I called back over my shoulder. "At noon. It's in the bylaws."

A few seconds later Alexander and I stood huddled together on his back porch. "You . . . think she'll . . . do it?" he asked me between breaths. Eyes closed, he leaned against the door.

"Nah," I said. "Once she thinks it over, she'll change her mind."

"Would *you* do it?" he asked.

"I don't *have* to do it, Alex. I'm already in the club."

The door behind Alexander opened so suddenly he landed on his rear in the kitchen. I found myself staring up into his stepfather's face. He had a baseball bat slung, like a club, over his shoulder. He did not look happy.

"You just scared your mother half to death!" he told Alexander. "Burglars!"

He grinned a little, first at Alexander then at me. His smile wasn't really all

that encouraging. "I assume you gentlemen have a good explanation for being out at this time of the night?" he said.

"I certainly hope so," I muttered under my breath.

He heard me. "Good. I'll just call your father first. You can tell us both at the same time." He lowered the bat and walked off in the direction of the living room.

"I hope you're satisfied," I whispered to Alexander. "Just look at the mess you've gotten me into."

If his dad hadn't come back into the kitchen just then, I think Alexander might have strangled me.

Captured!

I looked at my watch. Eleven fifty-seven.

"It could have been worse," Alexander told me. "We could've been grounded for the rest of the summer."

"I don't want to talk about it!" Eleven fifty-nine. If she was late, I could tell her it had to be noon exactly. Blame it on the bylaws.

Knock. Tap. Tap. Knock. Lizzie came in without being invited. The dog followed at her heels as usual.

"You aren't supposed to use the knock until you're in the club," I told Lizzie. "You gotta pass the initiation first. Unless you've changed your mind."

"I wouldn't be here if I changed my mind, would I?" she asked.

"Guess not," I said.

Two minutes later we were back behind Mrs. Mulligan's hedges, staring at her house. "This is your last chance to change your mind, Lizzie," I warned her.

"This is *your* last chance to come with me," she said. I knew a dare when I heard one. I pretended I didn't.

"I already told you. You gotta do it by yourself or it doesn't count. But we'll be right here if you need us. Just yell."

Natasha sat next to me, panting hot air on the back of my neck. "And take the dog, will you? You'll probably need her more than we will. Spooky old house like that. Crazy old lady and all."

"You'll come if I call, Bart?" Lizzie asked.

"You can count on the Gruesome Twosome. Right, Alex?"

"No problem," he said. I hoped I looked a little more sure about it than he did.

We held our breaths as Lizzie marched across old Mrs. Mulligan's lawn. She marched right up the stairs and banged on the door, louder than she had to.

The wooden door creaked open. There stood Mrs. Mulligan, in a bright pink sweatsuit. She had a flowered handkerchief tied around her curly red hair and a big wooden spoon in her hand. She laughed a hoarse, cackling sort of laugh.

"Maybe you'd like some of my special preserves, dearie?" she said. She motioned Lizzie inside with the spoon.

Natasha bounded onto the porch. I let out a sigh of relief. Then, instead of helping Lizzie, the dumb dog jumped up and licked old Mrs. Mulligan's face. Wagging her tail, she followed Lizzie inside. The big old door creaked shut again.

"Some protection!" I muttered. "Might as well have taken Hilda, Matilda, and Clyde."

Alexander's face was pale. "Fifteen minutes isn't so long, I guess," he said.

It seemed like an hour. And twenty-five minutes seemed like a year.

"You don't think she's in any trouble, do you?" Alexander asked.

"Nah. She'd. . . ."

OWWLLL! OWWLLL!

"What was *that*?" I said. We scrambled to our feet.

"It's the dog! Howling!" Alexander said. He started toward Mrs. Mulligan's house.

I grabbed his arm and held him back. "The dog can take care of itself," I said. "It's Lizzie I'm worried about."

"There she is!" Alexander pointed to Mrs. Mulligan's kitchen window.

A drape was pulled aside. I could see the familiar curly red hair. The window went up, just a crack.

"Alex! Bart!" Lizzie called in a horrible, screechy sort of voice. "I need you!"

The window went down, suddenly, with a bang. The drape fell back across the window. Lizzie disappeared. The dog howled again, twice.

"What do we do *now*?" Alexander asked me.

"I guess we, uh . . . go and get her, like we promised," I said. I hoped he'd try to talk me out of it.

He didn't. He started toward the house again.

"Wait," I said. "I've got a plan." I led the way to the back of the house. Alexander was mumbling and grumbling right behind me the whole way.

"Couldn't we just knock on the door like Lizzie did?" he asked when we got where we were going.

"Sure," I said. I lifted the cellar door slowly and quietly.

"And we could end up captured like Lizzie, too."

I peered down the cracked cement stairway leading into Mrs. Mulligan's basement. "Uh, after you," I said.

"Thanks," Alex said. "Thanks a heap."

The cellar looked a lot worse from the inside than it did when we were peeking in the window. It was dark, except for the broad shaft of light coming in through the open cellar doorway and the thinner beams filtering down from the single, iron-grated window.

The dirt floor was muddy. It pulled at our sneakers, making a sickening, sucking, grabbing sort of a noise. *Ffthtt! Ffthtt! Ffthtt!* The wall under the window was alive with slimy wet moss.

"Go on," I told Alexander. I pushed him ahead of me again. We inched our way toward the stairway leading up to the first floor.

"Tell me the plan again," he said.

I turned him around and held him by the shoulders. "We sneak up the stairs. We open the door. I create a diversion. Mrs. Mulligan comes out to see what the noise is all about. You grab Lizzie. You run out the back door. I run out the front. Nothing to it," I said.

A Sticky Situation

"You got it?" I asked Alexander.

"What if the door's locked?" he said.

I hadn't thought of that. "The door won't be locked. The door is never locked in the books." I motioned to the stairs. "Go on. I'm behind you all the way."

We tried to tiptoe. The steps creaked and groaned under our feet, especially Alexander's. We might as well have been a marching band. The door was locked when we got there.

"I told you. . . ."

I put my hand over his mouth. "You want Mrs. Mulligan to hear you?" I pointed to the stairs behind me. "Come on. We have to switch to plan B."

"What's plan B?" he asked.

I had no idea. "It starts with getting out of this basement," I whispered. "Then maybe we'll just go knock on the front door. Maybe we'll just say, 'Look here, Mrs. Mulligan, we know you've got. . . .' "

Creak! Bang! We grabbed each other and jumped about three feet in the air. Someone had closed the outside door to the basement.

I was thankful for the little bit of light that still came through the window. "Come on!" I yelled. I ran down the stairs, two at a time. "We gotta get to that door before. . . ."

Scrape. Click.

It was too late. Someone had slid the bolt and locked the door from the outside. We were trapped in Mrs. Mulligan's basement!

Alexander and I stood at the bottom of the stairs. "What's plan C?" he asked me.

I had to think fast. I led him across the cellar. "Plan C . . ." I pointed toward the top of the green, slimy wall. ". . . is you going out that window."

"*Me*?" he said. "I can't even reach that window."

"You can if we pile up those old papers," I said.

It took forever to move the stack of old newspapers from under the stairwell to under the window. "Up you go," I told Alexander. He was halfway up before it occurred to him. "What if the window doesn't open. What if the grate can't be moved?"

"Will you be quiet and climb!" I told him. "Those old grates probably pull right out. And watch where you're going. You're leaning an awful lot to the left. Alex!"

The papers went one way. Alexander went the other. The tower collapsed, scattering newspaper pages in all directions. Alexander hung from the window grate. His legs swung from side to side against the wall, smearing green slimy stains all over his white shorts. I guess it was a good thing that the grate couldn't be moved after all.

"Get me down from here, Bart!" he said. "I can't hang on much longer."

I got up under him so he could put his legs on my shoulders. "Let yourself down, easy." I said. "I've got you."

The next thing I knew we were lying in a heap on the floor. "Nice going," I said. "Another trip to the laundry room!"

"This is all your fault anyway." Alex scraped the mud off his hands and knees. "You and your plans."

Click. Creak.

Someone was opening the door at the top of the stairs. We scrambled out of the mud and huddled together under the stairwell, where the newspapers used to be.

Click. The light went on.

"Heh! Heh! Heh! Hee! Hee! Hee!"

Mrs. Mulligan was cackling her way down the stairs. She stopped, half-way down. On the step that was on the level of my nose. Somehow the white high-top sneakers with the red racing stripes didn't quite fit the spooky laugh or my idea of Mrs. Mulligan.

Please, God, don't let her find us! I prayed.

"My goodness!" she said loudly. "Look at that! First the door is open. Now the newspapers are all over the place. It must be that old ghost again. Just because he died in my cellar is no reason to keep on making a nuisance of himself."

Alexander looked like he was going to be sick. I put my fingers to my lips, warning him to be quiet. I pointed with my other hand to the white high-top sneakers. They were moving down the stairs again. We held our breaths.

Mrs. Mulligan stepped carefully across the muddy cellar to the far wall. The wall was full of shelves. The shelves were full

of jars. The jars were full of who knows what. Green gunk. Pink goop. Orange lumpy stuff. Sickening brown mush.

Mrs. Mulligan reached up and added the jars in her arms to the jars on the shelves. More green gunk.

She turned around and started back toward the stairs. Alexander and I ducked down, quick, as low as we could.

Mrs. Mulligan stopped half-way up. "Well, at least I don't see the snake," she said, talking as loudly as before. "I hate snakes. Especially *big* ones." She cackled a little and went on upstairs. She turned off the light and relocked the door behind her.

"*Snake?*" Alexander said as soon as she was gone. "*Ghosts and snakes?*" He took off, at a run, toward the outside doorway.

I was right behind him. We heaved our weight, together, against the wooden door, trying to break the lock and push it open.

Bang! Bang! Thump! Ouch! The cellar door wouldn't budge.

I rubbed my shoulder. Somehow it looked a lot easier when the detectives burst through doors on TV.

"What are we going to do, Bart?" Alexander sounded as upset as I felt.

I didn't get to answer the question.

Click. Thud. Click. The door to the first floor was pushed open. On went the light.

"Burglars, that's what it is!" said a familiar, raspy voice. "I'd better call the police. They know how to handle burglars."

Click. Slam. Click. The light went off. The door went shut. The lock turned again.

"My dad isn't going to appreciate this," Alexander said. "Arrested. As a burglar. In Mrs. Mulligan's basement. I will never be able to explain this if I try for a million years."

Bang! Bang! Bang! Somebody pounded on the old wooden door at the top of the stairway behind us.

"It's the cops!" I said. "Hide."

We ran back toward the stairwell. Moving into the shadows, I bumped my head against something smooth, and cool, and hard. More of Mrs. Mulligan's jars. All sliding off the shelf I'd knocked off its brackets.

CRASH! SMASH! The first couple of jars went crashing to the floor. Lumpy, squishy gunk splattered all over everything, including us.

"Catch them!" I yelled. "Before they all go!"

SMASH! POP! BANG! A half-dozen more jars slid off the shelf.

Behind us the cellar door creaked open. There wasn't a thing we could do. We stood there, holding up the shelf to keep the rest of the jars from falling into the slop at our feet.

Two to the Rescue

"Down there, officer. Burglars. A whole gang of them by the sounds of it. Drag them out of there. Throw them in jail."

"Jail?" Alexander whispered hoarsely.

"Shh," I told him.

"What's that, officer?" Mrs. Mulligan asked.

I couldn't hear the policeman. Mrs. Mulligan's answer was loud and clear. "You're right, officer. They may be armed and desperate. You'd better go for reinforcements. I'll keep the door locked."

Creak! Bang! Slide. Click.

We were locked in the basement again. With Mrs. Mulligan guarding the door. Waiting for the policeman to come back with reinforcements. I couldn't see Alexander's face very well. He wasn't armed, but I could bet he looked pretty desperate.

"Bart?" he whispered. He sounded pretty desperate, too. "I have to go to the bathroom."

I groaned. "If I ever complain about being bored again. . . ."

"Somebody's coming, Bart!"

The upstairs door opened again. Whoever it was didn't turn on the light. Something heavy barreled down the stairs.

Something cold and wet pressed up against my back. Something very furry breathed hot and heavy against my skin. A wet tongue licked the sticky gunk from my ankles. My knees felt weak. It was worse than I expected. The police had brought attack dogs!

I thought about letting go of the shelf, jars and all. But I was afraid to make any sudden moves because of the dog. Dogs get nervous when they sense you're afraid. I read that somewhere.

"Nice dog," I whispered. "I just love dogs." The dog nibbled at the goop on my knee. I wondered how nervous they got if you fainted.

"Natasha! Bart? Alex? Are you down there?"

I was never so glad to hear anyone in my life. "Lizzie! Over here! Quick!"

Hilda, Matilda, and Clyde would have gotten there quicker. Lizzie shined a flashlight on me and then on Alexander. She laughed as though we were the funniest thing she'd seen in years.

"I wish I had a camera!" she said.

"We gotta get out of here, Lizzie. Before the cops come," Alexander told her. "You gotta help us."

"I don't know," Lizzie said. "Maybe I will. Maybe I won't."

"What's that supposed to mean?"

"Natasha and I will have to take a vote first. To see if we really *want* to help you," Lizzie said. "Maybe we should just leave you here till the police come? It would make a great initiation. See if you're brave enough to join *our* club? The Terrific Two. Good name, huh?"

"*Lizzie!*" Alexander and I both pleaded at once.

"What do you think, Natasha?" Lizzie said, ignoring us completely. The dog barked.

"Am I in your silly club or not?" Lizzie asked me.

"Was there ever any doubt?" I smiled into the flashlight beam. "Why else would we have risked our necks to rescue you?"

She thought that was very funny. But she did find a couple of old clothes poles to prop up the shelf.

I let down my arms and rubbed my shoulders. "Thanks," I said.

"Now, let's get out of here! Mrs. Mulligan's guarding the outside door. We'll have to go through the upstairs."

Lizzie led the way with the flashlight. Alexander was right behind her. I was right behind him. The dog trailed at my ankles, mumbling and grumbling again. I tucked in my rear and tried to push Alexander forward a little faster. Suddenly, Lizzie stopped. The four of us plowed into one another at the bottom of the stairs.

"Look at that!" Lizzie said. "Just what I need! Mom's got a new housekeeper coming on Monday."

The flashlight beam fell between the steps, on the floor under the stairs. Right where Alexander and I had been hiding. At first I thought it was an old piece of garden hose. It stretched out, about six feet long, across the muddy floor. Then Lizzie walked around to the back of the stairs, bent down, and picked it up.

She whistled. "Hey, Bart, did you ever see such a beautiful. . . ."

Alexander, Natasha, and I were upstairs in a couple of seconds flat. I flung open the door and ran right into Mrs. Mulligan.

She had one hand on her hip. The other hand held an old-fashioned straw broom. She took a step forward. For a second I expected her to get on the thing and fly away. She tapped the bottom of the broom on a rubber floor mat. "Wipe your feet, young man," she said.

I scraped the bottom of my muddy sneakers on the mat. "I, uh . . . was just . . . sort of passing through . . . and, uh. . . ."

"Out of the way, young man," she said. She motioned me aside with her broom.

Alexander stepped onto the landing. He wiped his feet too.

Natasha didn't bother wiping her feet. She ran over to Mrs. Mulligan and held up a paw. Mrs. Mulligan leaned over and scratched the dog behind the ears. "No goodies now, Tasha," she said. "I've got burglars to deal with."

"We're not burglars, Mrs. Mulligan," I said. "We were just sort of. . . ."

Just then Lizzie came to the top of the stairs. She had something long, black, and shiny coiled around her arm. "Have you ever seen such a beautiful snakeskin, Aunt Millie?" she said.

I couldn't believe it. "*Aunt* Millie?" I said to Lizzie.

Lizzie nodded. "I tried to tell you."

I was annoyed. The whole thing had been nothing more than a joke, a trick. I grabbed Alexander by the arm. "Come on, Alex," I told him. "We're going home."

Mrs. Mulligan picked up her broom and shook her head. "You're not going any-where, young man."

The Fearsome Foursome

"This is getting to be a habit, Alex," I said. I pulled my wet clothes out of Mrs. Mulligan's washer and threw them into the dryer.

There I was. In my underwear again. In somebody else's laundry room. I set the dial and turned on the machine.

Mrs. Mulligan had fixed us a snack to eat while we waited. Muffins and preserves. She said she'd send some home with us for the church social too. Mrs. Mulligan was full of surprises.

The snack looked good. After cleaning up Mrs. Mulligan's basement, I was hungry. I smeared a glob of preserves on the muffin and raised it to my mouth.

Alexander grinned. "You know what the teenagers say," he reminded me.

I'd listened once too often to what the teenagers had to say. "Yeah," I said. "I know." I took a big bite. The muffins were as good as Mrs. Mulligan's brownies.

I was just about to have another big bite when somebody tapped at the door. "You can't come in," I said. "We're in our . . . uh, we're not ready."

The tapping continued. I peeked out the door. Something warm and wet licked my nose. Natasha ran over to the snack table and held up a paw.

"Nice dog," I said. I broke off a big chunk of my muffin and held it out to her.

"These are really good," I told Alexander. "You should get the recipe."

He nodded. "Add a little peanut butter to these blueberry muffins . . . a banana or two . . . and they wouldn't be half bad." He licked the preserves off his fingers.

"You know, Mrs. Mulligan isn't so bad either. It only took a couple of hours to clean up that mess. She could have called the cops. Or our fathers."

"I'd rather go to jail any day," I said.

Alexander swallowed his muffins. "Lizzie didn't have to help us, either. Especially after the way we treated her. And she did pass the initiation, Bart."

He was right. Lizzie had pitched in and helped us clean up the broken jars, spilled preserves, and scattered, muddy newspapers. It would have taken a lot longer without her.

I tossed the last chunk of muffin into the air. Natasha caught it before it hit the floor. Then she went over to the door and scratched to be let out again.

I was almost sorry to see her go. I stroked her smooth, soft fur. She felt a lot better than Hilda, Matilda, and Clyde. She licked my hand. I opened the door and she ran out into the hall.

I went over to the dryer and tested the laundry. Only slightly damp. I threw one pair of shorts and a shirt to Alexander and started putting on the others.

"You know," I said, "we really oughta get rid of those frogs. Before they croak."

Alex groaned at my dumb joke, but he agreed. "We can take them back to the pond tonight, right after dinner. We'll ask Lizzie to come too." He hesitated, one arm in, one arm out of his shirt. "If it's okay with you."

I thought it over. Lizzie *was* a lot of fun. She liked Barnaby Baines. She passed the initiation. And she helped us clean the basement even after we'd been sort of mean to her. If she could be forgiving, so could I. "Sure," I said. "Why not?"

A few hours later, we released Hilda, Matilda, and Clyde. They seemed to appreciate it. Then we went back to the clubhouse.

"You bring the paint?" I asked Alexander.

He pointed to the two cans in the corner, next to the old rocker Mrs. Mulligan had donated from her attic.

I let Lizzie do the honors herself. She painted over the NO GIRLS sign and underlined the NO TEENAGERS part in red.

I looked at HOME OF THE GRUESOME TWOSOME, painted across the door. "I guess we need to change the name of the club, too," I said.

"How about "Terrific Trio?" Lizzie suggested.

"Not awesome enough," I said. "How can we strike fear in the hearts of the teenagers with a name like that?"

I thought it over. "Fear. . .fearsome." I smiled. "How about the Fearsome Foursome?"

"Foursome?" Alex asked. "There are only three of us, Bart."

I fished in my pocket and pulled out the chocolate chip cookie I'd brought from home. I held it out in front of our new mascot. "If *you* think the name should be The Fearsome Foursome, raise your paw, Natasha," I said.

She did.

I gave her the treat and a pat on the head. Then I raised my hand. "Two votes for the Fearsome Foursome," I said.

Lizzie and Alexander raised their hands, too. And that was the end of that.